The Weight of the Minolta in Her Hand

poems by

Marianna Hofer

Finishing Line Press
Georgetown, Kentucky

The Weight of the Minolta in Her Hand

ACKNOWLEDGMENTS

Thanks to the editors of the following journals for publishing these poems:

Damselfly: The Apprentice Photographer Confesses This Much [online]
Earth's Daughters: The Apprentice Photographer Holds a Tiny Silence in Her
Hands
Freshwater: The Apprentice Photographer and One Theory of the Narrative
Kerf: The Apprentice Photographer Leaves the Lesser Ghosts Behind
Love & Ensuing Madness: The Apprentice Photographer & One Theory of Light
[online]
Paper Nautilus: The Apprentice Photographer & a History of the Daguerreotype
Perigee: The Photographer's Apprentice Lover [online]
RAG: A Childhood Story
The Ravensperch: The Apprentice Photographer Memorizes the Book of Light;
The Apprentice Photographer Stands in the Side Yard of Silence; The Apprentice
Photographer Thinks about Poetry [online]
San Pedro River Review: The Apprentice Photographer Falls in Love
Santa Fe Literary Review: The Apprentice Photographer at the Edge of the
Known World
Slant: The Apprentice Photographer Documents Love Carefully
Trajectory: The Apprentice Photographer Recounts This Story [online]

Publisher: Leah Maines

Editor: Christen Kincaid

Cover Art: Marianna Hofer

Author Photo: Dave Kent

Cover Design: Elizabeth Maines McCleavy

Printed in the USA on acid-free paper.
Order online: www.finishinglinepress.com
            also available on amazon.com

Author inquiries and mail orders:
Finishing Line Press
P. O. Box 1626
Georgetown, Kentucky 40324
U. S. A.

Table of Contents

for
Tom, in gratitude
&
Jon, wherever

In my view you cannot claim to have seen something until you have photographed it.
—Emile Zola

THE APPRENTICE PHOTOGRAPHER CHRONICLES

THE APPRENTICE PHOTOGRAPHER
FALLS IN LOVE

Her father and favorite uncle would,
not so much from curiosity but
simply because there they were, standing
at a door crooked on its hinges, walk
through the abandoned houses that,
hugged by lilacs and daylilies, rose up
from the woodlots or field edges.

She was a kid,
alternately almost spooked
by the stripped and emptied,
puzzled and concerned in the ones
where the still life left behind
spelled out daily life in
dirty spoons, broken spined books,
plaid shirts, muddy shoes dropped
after a day. Not a good or
a bad day, just any farm day
where someone mused aloud
'how much is wheat selling for?
Should I buy more milk cows? hogs?'

She never touched or carried
anything away with her, tried
not to, if possible, rearrange
history. She understood
not much of this was romantic
or tragic on a grand scale,
at times it was just
someone walked or ran away,
and that became the end.

She moved across state to
the flatlands, found empty
houses either settled into

tangled vines and brambles,
once cultivated flowerbeds
grown crazy, or else tied
to stretches of wheat or
soybeans sweeping at
the edges of a ragged yard.

She focuses precisely,
documents in black and white
loose wallpaper stirred by
a breeze, doors in degrees of
open or closed, window frames
full of glass, or wind, or latticed vines,
fallen ceilings, exposed lath work.

It all might seem so
clear, so visible here.
But she knows it's not.
To pick up and go, to stay,
to try again, who can
really expect the answers
to rise up in front of them?

One morning it just happens.
The door doesn't even close
right anymore, there's no soap
to wash the breakfast dishes.
And, just as in the minute before
the solid click of a camera shutter,
the story's probable end
comes into sharp sudden focus,
and it's now, now in
the lush language of light.

THE APPRENTICE PHOTOGRAPHER
RECOUNTS THIS STORY

Combines and tractors kick up chaff,
dust, headlights ragged streaks
across half shorn fields. The twilight
smells of sweet grain, dry air.

A two lane highway curves
through small farm towns full of
church steeples, neon bar signs.

She can't imagine going back to
any place like her hometown even
as the shapes of houses on her
childhood street, shortcuts downtown,
her father's hands on the steering wheel,
pieces from a series of incomplete
details, linger on.
                                        Out here
she can photograph pasts not
hers, pasts that suddenly found
themselves not exactly abandoned,
more likely inadvertently forgotten,
left behind in the rush to get on
to the next promise.

THE APPRENTICE PHOTOGRAPHER
AT THE EDGE OF THE KNOWN WORLD
for my father, Uncle Ernie & Aunt Matilda

By the time her aunt and uncle sold
the farm, moved to an old house on
one acre outside Apple Creek, she was
11 or 12, and her father and uncle had
provided stacks of practical instruction to
handle, in theory, whatever might rise up—
floodwaters, winter wheat—in front of her.

How to hold a camera. Why
she needed to hold it. To run
a milking machine, a rusted tractor.
Recognize the farm's played out,
get out before it's all gone to
wreck and ruin. That damn near
any situation, no matter the start,
can turn difficult at times. But
she needed to just buck up, go on,
there's never a question of not
doing, not finding a way, but
making it as best she can.

She wades into thigh high grass,
into the meticulous beauty of
this emptied farmhouse.

She can never bring herself to walk
in a door left ajar or swung open,
hinges cracked, instead content to aim
the Minolta through half open doors,
glassless windows, sure she never
wants to stand in the middle of
the intimate revelations left behind
carelessly or with full intentions, what
love or despair or flat out frustration
couldn't shove into a suitcase.

Redwing blackbird on a fencepost.
The shambles of the grass, wiry
roses, handfuls of white peonies,
mock orange grown boisterous.

Yellow iris drift at the far corner
of the property, beauty placed
deliberately where she has to look
a ways off down the road to find it.

She cried when the farm got sold.
Her uncle walked off so easily.
She didn't see then how anyone
could leave all that beauty, all
the redundant work and uncertainty
that kept it all going and seem to
never look back, ever regret anything.

She frames up a shot, glances
back over her left shoulder, a ritual
at every house.
                    Always she finds
only all that romantic notion so
hard to keep pristine and functional
without some heart breaking down
at any given moment.

THE APPRENTICE PHOTOGRAPHER
MEMORIZES THE BOOK OF LIGHT

3 miles from the High Level Bridge
sun shimmered against the 4 lanes as if
hundreds of tiny glass beads found
themselves dumped out on Main Street.

The street was pretty nearly deserted
for the middle of a warm day, only
a few cars, storefronts small but bright,
especially the boarded up ones.

And she drove along, just a kid, really,
on her way to somewhere, someone.

That day washes back not like
a dream, more as a set of wistful
snapshots, her 19 year old self
full of unstudied images.

                    *

You drive, bring her to this 3-way stop
at some edge of town where a field
spreads itself out in that late May sort
of way, pale green and luminous.

There's the silence between songs
on a CD, rattle of the gearshift
under your fingers, that slight weight
of a camera bag against her feet.

The sunlight sweeps
a curious hand against
the young wheat, that shy
honest light in your eyes.

THE APPRENTICE PHOTOGRAPHER
THINKS ABOUT HISTORY

an abandoned miniature golf course, Tiffin, Ohio
for Tom

Those first steps into the field,
the long overgrown yard, towards
a desolate structure, this time
a forgotten miniature golf course.
She feels her own breath, the weight
of the Minolta in her hand, silence
that really isn't silence, just
an absence that leans like
a quick stray cat at the ankles.

        Those first moments,
car turned off, key pulled from
the ignition, music stopped,
door slammed shut, it's as if
being struck deaf. Then
the shift of shoes against
grass or gravel, and the air,
even if it barely stirs, plies
a voice at her ear, curls
through her hair, hums off key
while the shutter clicks.

White glass shards scatter all over,
bits of fluorescent tubes that rusted
free from the towering overhead lights,
then fell, she assumes, one at
a time, the final corrosion severed
by wind, rain, the weight of
a mourning dove, or just
an ordinary day, the sound
a sudden fast thin explosion not
unlike expensive wine glasses
hurled against a sidewalk not
so much to be heard, just done.

In the surrounding unmowed field,
last year's Queen Anne's lace
skeletal in grass bent double
by its own weight, she looks

absently out across the distance,
the sound of a river just beyond
the road, the Minolta comfortable
in her left hand, film inside full
of hopeful waiting images.

She turns as if gradually waking
from a silent movie to find you, who
showed her this place, quiet by
toy fairways lost to ragged overgrowth.
She tries out a picture of you as
a young boy, awkwardly graceful,
child sized putter in your hands
in the shiny wordless light.

And she says your name.
Just like that.

THE APPRENTICE PHOTOGRAPHER
HOLDS A TINY SILENCE IN HER HAND

A fortuneteller, she thinks.
Basic knowledge about the future
might not be, some days, such
a bad idea. But she never knocks at
'Tarot Card Reader Open,' suspects any
advance information wouldn't turn her
back around the way she came.

She meets a percussionist reduced
to rhythm sticks. He wears three
perfect black teardrops tattooed
below his left eye, a trail that ends
just beyond his cheekbone.
He never speaks. His voice
she imagines an armchair in
a field, a 1940's stove. A field
of briars where a one story house
leans, front room full of books,
washers, dryers, shot out TV,
a shroud of winter bare vines runs
roof to floor. The question
she always asks, even as she
frames the shot. What unfolded
here. Predictably, he whispers
nothing in her hair, just a moment
of his hands at the small of her back.

The first time she ever speaks
to you, turns around, says hello,
you speak so softly a window,
glass scrubbed clean, falls open
somewhere you don't hear.
She slips in through that window,
starts over again then. She finds light
spilled along carved baseboards,
wallpaper now just pale patterns
loose in the breeze.

THE APPRENTICE PHOTOGRAPHER
AND ONE THEORY OF LIGHT

A small girl, 9 or 10, she'd be left by her folks at
the farm outside Blachleyville for a week or two,
go to church there with her favorite aunt.

She wonders now, when she thinks
of them, what, if any, denomination
the congregation was, if it mattered beyond
a chance to clean up, socialize, contemplate
different challenges for an hour or two.

Sunday school met in the bell tower
where once a yellow plate of
fresh sugar cookies sat on
a windowsill. Dusty morning sun
at an angle, thick bars of light
slashed across the pale cookies,
sugar crystals turned to prisms.
The room smelled of vanilla.

*

Blue February evening light
thick with the possibility of
late winter fog. At the corner
of Main and Crawford you shine
in the hazy mercury vapor light,
it falls like well worn velvet
on your shoulders.

You cross the street.
The air smells of melting snow.
She touches the sleeve of
your jacket, would scoop
the light, crumbling, indistinct,
into her hands, pour it
into yours if only she could.

The lush language of light.
The language of lush light.
Like love, here it is, falling
from nowhere in particular.

THE APPRENTICE PHOTOGRAPHER
CONFESSES THIS MUCH

The possums kick up a ruckus
under the kitchen floor again.
She stomps down over where
their heads must be. They keep
on hissing and snapping underfoot.
She stomps again. Silence.

Winter and cold have driven them
to shimmy into the crawlspace,
abandon the shed at the back fence
where they fought or loved, she's
not sure which this is, in peace.

The winter it snowed nearly
every week she finally grew tired
of the shovel in her hands.
She threw the fresh snow on
the previous weeks' accumulations,
precariously arranged piles that
didn't completely melt away
until one day in March
she woke, they were gone.

Anyway, it was winter, night,
unshoveled snow shone like
shattered glass, shimmered in
the hair that escaped her hood.

She conjectured there was
all this beauty in the man
who opened the door she
knocked at, who watched her
shake snow from hair, skirt,
that this time it would stay,
but even as she stood loosening

boot laces, she saw a series
of photos that looked perfect
as the shutter clicks, but later
tell no story worth repeating.

On a street by a junkyard of
slightly disarrayed cars, someone
either chose, or more likely,
given the neighborhood, found
themselves moved, trash bags tipped,
busted bed frame shoved into a bush.

A dining table and chairs on the porch
wait for breakfast to walk out
the flung open door, cereal and juice,
maybe even french toast, to appear.
In the curtained front room, a white
upright piano, paint job earnest,
brushstrokes labored, obvious.

She stands on the sidewalk, Minolta
in her left hand, recognizes that
blend of salvation and frustration,
that cross of willingness tempered
by an awareness the door will, most
likely, slam hard over and over,
maybe never stop.

One near perfect shot. The piano floats,
a conjured image in low light behind
the promised open air breakfast,
a well intentioned attempt to
salvage what might have
splintered apart one last time.

THE APPRENTICE PHOTOGRAPHER
THINKS ABOUT POETRY

Sharp small lights, wistful
in their solitudes, kiss
at the edges of uncombed
woodlots far back from
this unlit road, landscape
unrolled bolts of just
washed black muslin.

A handful of pennies slung
onto the ragged asphalt,
a copper constellation that
tells some mythic moment
gone awry between mortals
or celestial beings, a cautionary
tale to pay attention to what
could possibly go wrong,
those involved suddenly
not themselves ever again.

Disheveled slight houses
crowd a thin street. Tiny plain
birds whir in empty bushes.
White Christmas lights flicker,
loop over the lower branches
of a stunted sugar maple.

Late February. The day
a freshly sharpened knife blade
flat along her cheekbones.

THE APPRENTICE PHOTOGRAPHER
AND ONE THEORY OF THE NARRATIVE

The wind. That lonely lovely hollow note
come through dense pines. She lowers
the Minolta, shifts her weight, listens.

The house she kneels in front of long ago left
paint, window glass, screens, behind. Now
thin plywood snugly boards up doors and windows,
keeps spring dust, winter damp, from loosening
floorboards, warping door frames, staining baseboards.

She thinks about words she could use, holds
suspiration against susurration, prefers
that deep sigh over a whispering sound.

How far out into the country, away from a studio
drenched in off white light, stacked in papers and
words, prints and negatives, to here, a whole land
scape rinsed clean of sharp colors all the way across
a picked over cornfield to a static horizon line.

Every so often one of these houses
shifts hard, collapses under its own
lassitude or burns in a careless moment.

Too often ghosts walk past a doorway, glance
into a window, just a white shape in the corner
of an eye that doesn't stop, doesn't deliver
the story because there really isn't one, just
that restless need to walk again on solid ground.

THE APPRENTICE PHOTOGRAPHER
& A HISTORY OF THE DAGUERREOTYPE

A door blooms like a wall of shy moonflowers.
Smoke stained light the length of the bar
the random kiss at her cheekbone.
Conversations fall around her, through her
fingers like pale confetti.

The familiar kiss smack of a cue ball at the break,
that patient way scattered balls roll to a stop
on thin green felt, Elvin Bishop's 'Fooled
Around and Fell in Love,' some softly spoken
advice about the best pocket to try for.

She once was only just the girl with the painter,
gone now, who she trailed through luminous
back alleys, whitewashed doors. She lingered
at his studio, his thin hands flecked with
fresh oil paint. Or she'd find him
idlely flipping a deck of worn cards,
solitaire in a coffeeshop.

A friend's hand, just that sudden
simple touch on her lower back
to slow her as she walks towards
a bar's back door, a night sky
turned inside out, clouds
stretched to fit snug,
hold this light steady.

THE APPRENTICE PHOTOGRAPHER
DOCUMENTS LOVE CAREFULLY
for Chris Kohli

Frayed paper scraps, folded index cards,
unsticky sticky notes, sheets from
steno notepads, date books, neatly
printed, scribbled, cursive looped wide
or precisely controlled, pencil, pen, in
the grass, the streets, the sidewalk cracks.

She never picks them up or looks
too long at the handwriting, just
apprehensive enough she might find
his recipe for gesso, the balance
of blues to greens, a list of new wines,
a sonata title he wanted to play on
the piano in a bar's back room.

Behind expensive blinds in
second floor windows, pale
yellow light. Angular white walls
fade to washed out sky blue
as dark sinks in. He worked,
paintbrush and all the knowledge
she was curious for precise
in his slender hands. She
learned viridian green, cerise,
cadmium yellow, cerulean blue,
every exotic color possible.

When photography still felt new,
still a luxury and an ordeal, often
the local photographer was
brought in to record the coffined
dead, no need to brace them,
remind them not to smile, no

worry they'd tire of the pose, shift
weight from one foot to another,
for example, and blur the exposure.
How, she wonders, in those
moments, did the photographers
stop the tremble in their hands?

Decades of disuse, of decay,
hang off defunct exposed
electric wires, from strips of
loose decorative plaster trim
on the Jones Building's third floor.
She's never been all alone
here in his studio, the one
cleared room, pristine northern
exposure through grimy high
narrow cathedral windows.

The natural light he prized begins
to fade, the studio takes on
the pattern of his more elaborate
still lifes. In the doorway
she sets up the tripod, snaps
the legs into place, leans to
settle the Minolta's focus,
shutter release cable looped
through her self-assured fingers.

A last lonely office, a lovely office,
for the dead. The impermanence of
existence, of creation, a record of both
the photographed and the photographer.

THE APPRENTICE PHOTOGRAPHER
LEAVES THE LESSER GHOSTS BEHIND

Beneath slender beech and maples,
young and beautifully straight, light falls
luminous and grainy through the branches,
unfolds carelessly over piles of bumpers,
stacks of doors, rusted anonymous frames
scattered all about, spindly errant seedlings.

Muffled voices drift, a door bangs at
the junkyard's far edge. Cars, mainly
late model Fords in various states
of dismemberment, shine out from
heavy grass like misinformed fireflies.

Goldfinches, reckless and sharp, hurl
themselves up into sun bleached air,
their trajectories too dizzying to trace
against the sky. The humidity reeks
of old metal, dry motor oil.

She loves b&w film. How it holds tight
to image after image, that eager tension
always there inside the mechanics of
the Minolta in her hands, a faintly
electric, silvery exhalation that rises
gracefully up through her ribcage.

The hardtop '58 Thunderbird, once
a yellow borrowed from a Jujubes box
back in a past now long divorced
from drivers and roadways, rests easy
in a bright stand of slender beeches,
a Renaissance angel settled down,
finished with the excitement of wings, done
transporting amazement and revelation.

She sizes it all up in a wide angle lens,
then lowers the Minolta, practices
her one virtue of patience, waits
on grainy light to shift just a fraction
of an inch more to the right, sprawl
around the pale luminous beech trees,
the Thunderbird's left rear quarterpanel,
those delicate filigrees of rust there.

THE APPRENTICE PHOTOGRAPHER
STANDS IN THE SIDE YARD OF SILENCE

The solid certain weight in
her hand. The man who first
handed her his 35mm SLR,
a camera so far removed
from the typical Kodaks in
their slick plastic cases.

At the odd moment, wind calls
through an open field or
from around the corner of
some bare boned house,
conjures up Jon, if he married,
had kids, documented every
sunny day, or if the drugs
finally ate him alive.

Or if, as she'd done once,
he simply put up the cameras,
willed himself to not need a lens
to see small beauty, potential
heartbreaker, there in front
of him, that passion gone too,
exploded, burned, buried.

The wind, tactile and eager,
leans up against her. There's
the sound of a loose door
smacking over and over
against a wall somewhere
not so far away, a dog's yip,
car tires too far off to ever be
seen clearly, sometimes
scraps of voices snagged
by a fast cross breeze.

In those odd moments, he turns
into an insistent glimmer on
busted window glass, splintered
front porch she knows better
than to step up on. Vines knit
through concave roof, buckled
walls, over railings. She
stands thigh deep in tangled
frost burned grass, can see
clean through this house,
then forgets him again.

She pulls stick-me-tights
from scarf, sweater, even
her hair, camera strap, tries
to get them out whole, later
finds embedded shards,
seeds tenaciously hopeful
they've found a place to
start again, the past just that,
all the mistakes, stupid decisions,
left there in the slow decay
neglect brings, left for her
to document this day in
a shroud of bright sunlight.

THE APPRENTICE
PHOTOGRAPHER SPEAKS
FOR HERSELF

THE PHOTOGRAPHER'S APPRENTICE LOVER
for Jon

My first lover
taught me to hold
the weight of
a 35mm SLR camera in
the palm of my hand,
to focus, shoot, as if
nothing else meant
a thing, could ever
match what was in
the lens, the red light
of the darkroom.

Mute black and white
stories, dead end
streets, materialized in
the developer, filled sheets
of photographic paper,
reflected his silent
eye until the prints dried,
hung up like so much
common midwest laundry.

He was the first
photographer I'd
ever met. At 18
I wanted any world
that could open wide,
swallow me down, so
I found one that would
with a solid click of
a shutter, a film advance
lever pulled steady
against my thumb.

I took myself
and a camera down
a steep gorge I
couldn't climb out
of, balanced on
a flimsy bridge over
an ice jammed river
so cold my fingers
and shutter froze,
                    finally
stopped by the slant light
at the door to a failed
greenhouse, broken glass,
vines, tools, tumbled all
about, dislodged panes
still hanging from
rusted metal trusses

with the silence of
an unmade bed,
a darkroom just as
the image comes
into focus, but it's
all wrong, the final
seconds of love.

A CHILDHOOD STORY
for my father and Uncle Ernie & Aunt Matilda

One full of my father,
an uncle, me, and a house
set back, abandoned, in
a clearing. One of those
where you walk in to find
dolls, a plaid shirt, books
tossed to the floor, dishes
in the sink, the last meal
crusted on, a fork still
on the table. Neither
my father or uncle stopped
as they walked through.

This was nothing new. What
made them curious waited
at the edge of the gone
to tangled garden, hoes
rusted and rotted. Yellow
raspberries, a bush
loaded with pale amber.
Like any good 9 year old,
I didn't get it. What
my father and uncle saw
there. Or didn't see.

Is it the failure, or
just the fear
that sets someone
off, lets them
turn their back to
a sure thing, or,
worse yet, to
rare beauty, and
vanish empty handed
into the world again.

Marianna **Hofer** worked on her writing and B&W film photography in Studio 13 in the historic Jones Building in downtown Findlay, OH. She published her poems and stories in various literary journals, and her B&W photography hung in local juried shows and local eateries. *Barns*, a chapbook from O2 Press, was published in 1982, and *A Memento Sent by the World*, a full length collection from Word Press, was published in 2008.

www.ingramcontent.com/pod-product-compliance
Lightning Source LLC
LaVergne TN
LVHW051613080426
835510LV00020B/3265